Severo Ochoa

by Gregory Garretson

Raintree

Chicago, Illinois

Printed and bound in the China by South China Printing Company.
07 06 05
10 9 8 7 6 5 4 3 2 1

Library of Congress Cataloging-in-Publication Data:

Garretson, Gregory.
  Severo Ochoa / Gregory Garretson.
     p. cm. -- (Hispanic-American biographies)
  Includes bibliographical references and index.
  ISBN 1-4109-1298-1 (hc) -- ISBN 1-4109-1306-6 (pb)
  1. Ochoa, Severo, 1905- 2. Biochemists--Spain--Biography--Juvenile literature. I. Title. II. Series.
  QP511.8.O34G37 2005
  612'.015'092--dc22

                         2004025314

Acknowledgments
The publisher would like to thank the following for permission to reproduce photographs:
p.4, Getty Image/Pictorial Parade; p.14 Corbis/Archivo Iconografico; pp.18, 43, 45 AP Wide World Photo; pp.20, 28, 38, 48, 53 Corbis/Bettman; p.24 Corbis/E.O.Hoppe; pp.27, 30, 34, 37 Corbis/Hulton-Deutsch Collection; p.40 Photodisc; p.56 Getty Image/Express Newspapers; p.59 The Nobel Foundation.

Cover photograph: AP World Wide Photo.

Every effort has been made to contact copyright holders of any material reproduced in this book. Any omissions will be rectified in subsequent printings if notice is given to the publisher.

Some words are shown in bold, **like this**. You can find out what they mean by looking in the glossary.

Contents

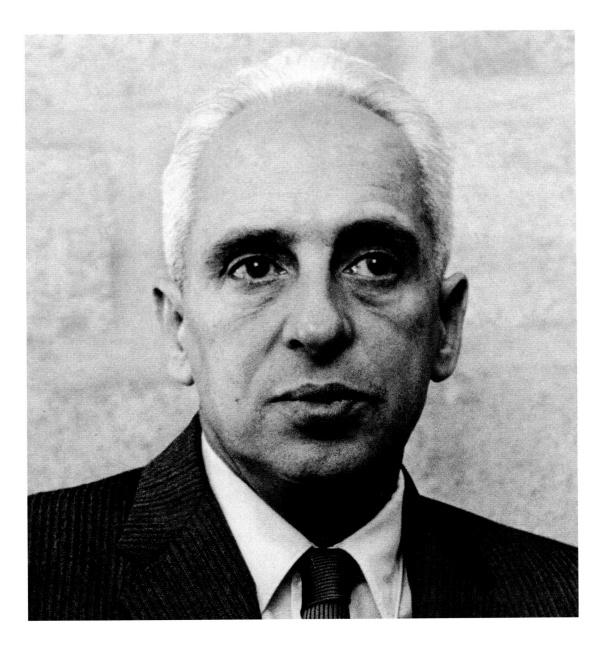

This photograph of Severo Ochoa was taken in 1945.

Introduction

Have you ever wondered how your body works? Or how eating a sandwich gives you the energy to go out and play a game of soccer? Why do people in the same family often look alike? Severo Ochoa was a very important scientist who was interested in finding the answers to these kinds of questions. From a very young age, Ochoa was sure that he wanted to be a scientist. Little did he know as a boy growing up in northern Spain that one day he would be one of the most important scientists in the world. Or that he would make discoveries that would earn him the Nobel Prize, the greatest honor a scientist can get!

Ochoa's path from a small town in Spain to becoming a scientist recognized all over the world was not an easy one. He had to move several times, sometimes in search of better opportunities for work, but other times to escape from war. But Ochoa always had two important things to keep him going: his wife, Carmen, who supported him, and his **determination** to work hard and make important discoveries in the science he loved.

Severo Ochoa was born in a small town in Spain in 1905. At a young age, he decided that he wanted to be a scientist. He went to medical school in Spain and started learning how to be a **biologist**. A biologist is someone who studies how the parts of plants and animals work. Ochoa worked with some of the most important biologists living at that time.

Like many people of his time, Ochoa was forced to leave his home because of war. First, there was a war in Spain, and then war broke out across Europe. Ochoa kept escaping from war and trying to continue his work. Finally, he and his wife fled to the United States, where they lived for many years. There he became a truly great scientist. He helped begin a new science, called **biochemistry**. Biochemistry is the study of the chemistry of living things, in particular the tiny structures in the body called cells. Ochoa also became the head of a university department in New York City.

One of Ochoa's greatest achievements was being awarded the Nobel Prize for Medicine in 1959. At that moment, he realized he was one of the very best scientists in the world. Ochoa dedicated his whole life to science, to his wife, Carmen, and to teaching young students who wanted to become scientists. He was a great inspiration to many people, who saw what hard work and a strong interest in science could achieve.

The Nobel Prize

In the early 1900s, the Swedish inventor Alfred Nobel decided to use his fortune for the good of all people. Nobel had invented dynamite, and he wanted to ensure that important inventors, scientists, and artists received the support that they would need in order to achieve their goals. He made sure that, after his death, prizes would be given to people who had managed to do important things to improve our world.

Nobel created a prize for various categories. Great writers would get the Nobel Prize for Literature, people who had done things for world peace would get the Nobel Peace Prize, and scientists who had made important discoveries would get the Nobel Prizes for **Physics**, **Chemistry**, and Medicine. Even world leaders, such as former U.S. President Jimmy Carter, have received the Nobel Prize.

More than 100 years later, Nobel Prizes are still awarded each year. Apart from the honor of receiving the prize, winners get a gold medal and a large amount of money. Since Alfred Nobel was Swedish, the Nobel Prize ceremony takes place in Stockholm, the capital of Sweden. The King of Sweden gives out the prizes at this very impressive event.

This is a map of Spain. Severo Ochoa grew up in Luarca, a town in the region of Asturias in Spain.

Chapter 1:
The Boy from Luarca

In the north of Spain, there is a green and mountainous region called Asturias, which stretches along the coast of the Atlantic Ocean. Where the mountains meet the sea, there is an ancient town called Luarca, with a port where ships leave to cross the ocean. In this town, in a large house with a beautiful garden, Severo Ochoa was born. His father, Severo Ochoa Pérez, was a lawyer and businessman who had lived in Puerto Rico and started an import-export business that brought in a fair amount of money. He and his wife, Carmen de Albornoz y Liminiana, had seven children, the youngest of whom they named Severo, after his father.

Severo Ochoa de Albornoz was born on September 24 in 1905. (In Spain everyone has two last names, one from their father and one from their mother. So young Severo got the first of his father's two last names, Ochoa, and the first of his mother's, de Albornoz.) Young Severo had many health problems and was carefully looked after by his mother, his grandmother, and his older sisters. He loved to spend time alone reading. But in a house with such a large family, it was not easy to find privacy.

So Ochoa would go outside to the garden, or to a little house where garden tools were kept, to sit and read adventure stories. Soon he started to take as much interest in the plants and animals of the garden as in his books. He began to go on long walks in the countryside around his home, and to explore the beach at low tide, studying the many sorts of plants and animals that lived there. Ochoa was fascinated by the natural world, and became interested in learning how it worked. Little did he know that this interest would one day lead him to becoming a great scientist.

Loss of His Father

Ochoa enjoyed his life in the big house, reading and exploring. But suddenly, when he was seven years old, his father died. The family did not know what to do. Luckily, they continued to receive money from his father's company, but Ochoa's mother, Carmen, was not well, and her doctor suggested that she should go somewhere warmer until her health got better.

Ochoa's oldest brother, Antonio, left to work in Puerto Rico, and his other brother, Luis, went to study law in Oviedo, the capital of Asturias. The rest of the Ochoa family decided to move to Málaga, in the south of Spain, at least until Carmen was in better health. And so Ochoa, his mother, and his sisters Dolores, Manola, and Concha packed their possessions and prepared for the long trip to the south.

Málaga is a city on the coast of the Mediterranean Sea, in the region called Andalusia. The weather was very different from what Ochoa had been used to in the north. While Asturias was cool and humid, Andalusia was hot and dry. Ochoa had never felt such heat as he experienced under the pounding sun of the south.

But Ochoa soon got used to his new surroundings. He started to go to school in Málaga and made new friends. His classmates liked him because he was friendly, easy to talk to, and never said anything bad about anyone. He and his friends would explore the neighborhoods of the city and go down to the harbor to visit the ships that had come from far-away places.

School in Málaga

At an early age, Ochoa became interested in photography. His brother Antonio gave him a camera so he could take pictures. Cameras weren't very common in those days, and Antonio showed Ochoa how to set up his own darkroom, where he developed his film and printed pictures. Ochoa's friends were very impressed with his room full of chemicals, lights, and containers. Working in the darkroom may have started Ochoa's interest in doing experiments in the laboratory, which is how he would spend much of his adult life. A laboratory, or lab, is a place where scientists work. It contains all sorts of specialized machines that scientists use for conducting experiments.

When Ochoa started high school in Málaga, he started taking a serious interest in science. Science is the study of how things work in the world. There are many types of science. For example, chemistry is the study of chemicals, which are the substances that make up everything from water to plants to humans. **Biology** is the study of living things, such as plants and animals, and their parts. Scientists are people who study the things in the world, trying to figure out how they work.

Ochoa had an excellent chemistry teacher who inspired him to start doing experiments on his own. He sometimes got into trouble with his family by mixing acid in the house and producing all sorts of terrible-smelling fumes!

Ochoa was a very talented and hard-working student. He studied not because he had to, but because he liked to. He had a tremendous curiosity about everything. His favorite subject was biology. He wanted to learn about how the various parts of the body work.

Becoming a Scientist

When Ochoa finished high school, he decided to continue his studies at a university. A university, also called a college, is a school for advanced studies after high school. His family wanted him to study engineering and learn how to build things. But Ochoa decided to study medicine because he wanted to become a doctor.

But Ochoa didn't want to be a typical doctor; he wanted to be a scientist. There are two kinds of doctors in medicine: **physicians**, who treat patients, and **medical researchers**, who do experiments in laboratories. Ochoa wanted to do research in a laboratory, and make discoveries about biology. But in Spain at that time, the only way to study biology was to study medicine. So Ochoa decided to go to medical school. He was only seventeen years old, but he knew what he wanted to do. He was determined to become a great scientist.

Santiago Ramón y Cajal was an important scientist and professor at the University of Madrid.

Chapter 2:
In the Footsteps of Ramón y Cajal

Knowing that studying medicine was a step on his way to becoming a biologist, Severo Ochoa prepared himself for medical school. He already knew where he wanted to study: the University of Madrid, where the great scientist Santiago Ramón y Cajal was a professor. A professor is a teacher at a university. Ramón y Cajal had won the Nobel Prize for Medicine. He was one of Ochoa's greatest heroes, and Ochoa wanted nothing more than to study with this brilliant scientist. So he left Málaga and moved to Madrid, in the middle of the country, the capital and largest city in Spain.

One of the biggest disappointments of Ochoa's life came when he arrived in Madrid and learned that Ramón y Cajal had just retired and would not teach any more. Ochoa would never be able to study with his hero! But he decided to continue with his plan to study at the University of Madrid. He quickly saw that there were other good professors there who he could learn from. Many of them had learned from Ramón y Cajal themselves. Ochoa knew that becoming a great scientist involved learning from other great scientists. Because of this, he paid very close attention to the lectures of his teachers and read all the books he could find by famous biologists.

Santiago Ramón y Cajal

Dr. Santiago Ramón y Cajal is one of the most important Spanish scientists ever, and one of the most important figures in the study of anatomy. Anatomy is the study of the different parts of the body. Ramón y Cajal studied the tissues, or materials, that the body is made of. He discovered that the neuron, or nerve cell, is the basic unit of the nervous system. The nervous system includes the brain and all of the cells that help us feel, see, taste, smell, and hear.

Ramón y Cajal was born in 1852 and worked at many different universities in Spain: in Zaragoza, Valencia, Barcelona, and Madrid. In 1906, he was awarded the Nobel Prize for his discoveries about the neuron. In 1920, a school was created in Madrid and named after Ramón y Cajal: the Cajal Institute, where Cajal himself worked until his death in 1934. He inspired generations of Spanish students to become scientists and to continue the study of anatomy.

Experimental Biology

Ochoa knew that there were not many people doing **experimental biology** in Spain. Experimental biologists learn about how the body works by doing laboratory experiments. There were many great scientists in other countries who he wanted to learn from. But their books were not usually translated into Spanish, so he tried to read them in French and English, which was very difficult for him.

Ochoa was a very good student. He spent most of his time studying and doing experiments. When his friends went out to go dancing or see movies, Ochoa often stayed alone in the laboratory. He shared an apartment with his brother Luis, and Ochoa wanted to perform experiments at home, too. But his brother would not let him. So Ochoa and a friend of his rented a room in a different neighborhood where they brought materials for doing experiments. They would go there in the evenings, after their classes, to continue working.

However, they were in for a surprise! When the neighbors saw the young men coming and going with strange equipment, such as chemicals, glass slides, and test tubes, they got nervous. They reported Ochoa and his friend to the police, who came to search their room. The police saw that they weren't doing anything wrong, so they left them alone.

This picture shows Ochoa in a lab in 1959.

A Promise to His Mother

A terrible shock came to Ochoa when, one day, his mother suddenly died. It was during a school vacation, and Ochoa was at home visiting his family in Luarca. He was in the garden reading, as usual, when his sisters came running. Their mother had just collapsed. Ochoa got into their car and drove to get the doctor. By the time he returned with the doctor, his mother had died.

Ochoa and his brothers and sisters had now lost both parents. They buried their mother in the cemetery in Luarca, overlooking the sea. People say that Ochoa, standing over the grave of his mother, cried "Mother, I promise never to stop working so that you will be proud of your son!"

Ochoa worked his whole life to become a great scientist. This photograph shows him at New York University Medical School Lab in 1959.

Chapter 3:
Becoming a Scientist

Ochoa fulfilled his promise to his mother. He returned to Madrid, determined to become a great scientist and make important discoveries. He threw himself into his work. Ochoa's teachers quickly saw that he was a very intelligent and hard-working student.

One teacher in particular, Dr. Juan Negrín, took Ochoa on as an assistant and taught him a tremendous amount about science, and especially about biology. Dr. Negrín was a brilliant and very likeable scientist, and Ochoa later said that he had learned more from Negrín than from anyone else.

Ochoa was such a good student that he was put in charge of groups of younger students. He also made money to support himself by giving private lessons to other students. However, while Ochoa was doing his studies, he had to take time out for military service. In Spain, both at that time and today, most young men have to spend a short time at around the age of 20 training for the military, in case there is a war and they are called upon to fight. This is still common in many countries in Europe that do not have large armies. Ochoa did not mind doing the military training because he got a lot of exercise, which improved his health. However, he was happy that he did not have to fight in a war.

One summer, Ochoa got the opportunity to take his first trip to another country. He went with three friends from medical school to France. Ochoa had studied French and English, but he did not speak either language well. He thought it was important to improve his language skills so he could read scientific articles in those languages. So he and his friends took a train to Paris and stayed there for a month, studying French.

Ochoa continued to work hard in the laboratory. He was particularly interested in how muscles work. For example, he wanted to know what chemical processes make them contract and expand. He performed many experiments and read everything he could find on the subject. He was particularly interested in the work that a scientist in Scotland was doing. He wrote to that scientist, Dr. Noel Paton, and asked if he could go there and work in his laboratory the next summer. Dr. Paton wrote back and said that Ochoa was welcome to come to Scotland.

Travel to Scotland

And so, in the summer of 1927, Ochoa made his second trip out of the country. He took a long train ride to Paris, and then another train to the English Channel. He crossed the channel in a boat and arrived in England. It was his first time in an English-speaking country, and Ochoa was amazed at how difficult it was for him to understand everyone! His English wasn't very good, but he communicated with people by writing notes and showing them. He traveled through England to Scotland, which is north of England. In Glasgow, Scotland, he met Dr. Paton and started working in his laboratory.

Ochoa had a very good experience in Glasgow. He learned a lot in the laboratory and also improved his English, which would be very useful to him later. In Dr. Paton's laboratory, he studied frogs. He learned so much in his experiments that he wrote his first article for publication, which Dr. Paton sent to a group of important scientists called the Royal Society of London. It was accepted and published. That means that the article appeared in a scientific journal, which is like a magazine for scientists. When scientists make discoveries, they write about them in articles, which are published in journals.

When Ochoa returned to Madrid, he was very excited to have published an article, and also to have learned a lot of English. He got in touch with his friend who he had shared the home

Ochoa spent the summer of 1927 working in a lab at the University of Glasgow in Scotland. This picture shows Glasgow during the 1920s.

laboratory with, and suggested that they write an article and try to have it published in an American journal. They wrote about the methods they had developed for studying muscles and sent the article to the *Journal of Biological Chemistry* in the United States, which was a very popular and important journal.

To their delight, the article was accepted, and was soon published. They had published an article in an important American journal! Little did Ochoa know that one day, he would be an American scientist, and one of the people in charge of that very journal!

Ochoa continued to work in the laboratory, and started to write articles for Spanish journals. Soon a professor at the university came to him and asked if he would help write a textbook for beginning medical students. The subject would be biochemistry, which was considered a new science at the time. Biochemistry is the study of the chemical processes in the bodies of plants and animals. Ochoa realized that he was one of the best people to write the book, and he accepted. The book was a big success, and Ochoa's reputation grew among scientists.

By this time, Ochoa was in a big hurry to finish his studies so he could spend all his time doing research. He took as many classes as he possibly could, and got high grades in almost all of them. Soon he would take his exams and become a doctor. But he did not consider his education to be complete. He had a lot more to learn if he was going to make important discoveries.

Going to Germany

Ochoa had read a lot about the work of a scientist in Germany named Dr. Otto Meyerhof. Meyerhof was a very important biologist who had won the Nobel Prize at a young age for his important research on muscles. In early 1929, Ochoa asked Dr. Meyerhof for permission to go to Berlin in northeastern Germany and work in his laboratory. Dr. Meyerhof said yes, and Ochoa left for Germany.

When he arrived in Berlin, Ochoa was very impressed with Dr. Meyerhof's laboratory. It had very modern equipment, and there were many excellent researchers working there. The only problem was that Ochoa hardly knew any German. Luckily, Dr. Meyerhof knew some English, so they were able to communicate. But Ochoa studied German until he was able to talk to all the other scientists in German. Now he had learned three foreign languages!

Crossing the Atlantic

After working for a few months in Berlin, Ochoa had the opportunity to attend a **conference** in Boston, Massachusetts, in the United States. A conference is a large meeting where people who study the same thing can make presentations to each other and exchange information. Ochoa was very excited to visit the United States for the first time in his life.

Ochoa worked with Otto Meyerhof (center) for several months at his lab in Berlin, and later in Heidelberg, Germany.

In the 1920s, traveling across the Atlantic meant spending several days on a ship. When Ochoa boarded the ship, he was amazed to learn that there were many famous scientists on board from many different countries, and all of them were going to the conference in Boston! Ochoa was inspired by being in the company of such important figures.

In order to travel to the United States, Ochoa had to cross the Atlantic Ocean on a passenger ship similar to this one.

The conference was a big success, and then Ochoa was able to travel around and visit a few places in the United States and Canada, including New York City, Albany, Toronto, and Montreal. He also saw Niagara Falls, the giant waterfall on the border between the United States and Canada. Ochoa enjoyed visiting North America, but did not realize he would soon be living there.

Back to Europe

After a long trip back to Europe on another ship, Ochoa returned to Madrid and prepared for his exams. If he passed them, he would be a doctor! He studied for several weeks, and then, on September 27, 1929, he took his exams and passed. He finally had his medical **degree** and was a doctor, at the age of only 24!

But Ochoa didn't want to be a physician and see patients. Instead, he was eager to continue the research on muscles he had been doing with Dr. Meyerhof. In December, of that year, he went back to Berlin, where he experienced the coldest weather he had ever known. It was so cold that as he was walking along the street with a friend one night, his friend's nose actually began to freeze!

Luckily, Dr. Meyerhof was moving his laboratory to Heidelberg, in the west of Germany, where it wasn't so cold. Ochoa went with him and continued his work there. He learned a tremendous amount from Dr. Meyerhof, who Ochoa later said was one of the biggest influences on him as a scientist. Ochoa began to get exciting results from his experiments, and he published his first article in German. However, little did he know that his life was about to be turned upside down by war.

Severo and Carmen Ochoa left Spain in 1936, when civil war erupted. This photograph was taken in 1937 and shows the Nationalists, one of the two sides fighting in the civil war, waving their flags and rifles for the camera. The Nationalists took control of Spain in 1939.

Chapter 4:
The Shadow of War

When Ochoa returned to Spain, the country was in a very unstable condition. The old government had collapsed, and many people were arguing about what kind of government should be formed to replace it. Ochoa's teacher, Dr. Negrín, left the university to become involved in politics. He became an important figure in one of Spain's political movements.

Falling in Love

Ochoa went back to Asturias to spend the summer with his family. There he met a young woman named Carmen Cobián, who he had known as a child. Carmen's parents had been good friends with Ochoa's parents, and their sisters had also been friends. Now, when Ochoa saw Carmen again, he was suddenly struck by how interesting and beautiful she was. They started to spend time together, and before long, Ochoa realized that he had fallen in love. They decided to get married the next year.

However, Ochoa had to return to Madrid to continue his research, and Carmen stayed in Asturias with her family. They were only able to see each other from time to time. Ochoa worked all year in the laboratory. Then, in July of 1931, Carmen and Severo were married back home in Asturias. The two went for a brief honeymoon, driving along the coast in a new American car. Then they went back to Madrid, so that Ochoa could continue with his work.

Carmen's Dedication

Carmen knew that Ochoa was a scientist completely dedicated to his work. And she knew that by marrying him, she was promising to follow him wherever his work took him. She happily accepted this adventure, and from then on she and Ochoa were never separated. She became the most important person in his life, and a big influence on his career.

Before long, Ochoa decided that he should leave Spain again and learn from scientists in other countries. This time, he decided to travel to England to work with the scientists Harold Dudley and Sir Henry Dale. So Severo and Carmen moved to England, living outside the capital city of London.

During Ochoa's time in England, Dr. Dudley introduced him to the study of **enzymes**. Enzymes are substances in the body that speed up chemical reactions. For example, they control the digestion of food. Without enzymes, the body would not work at all.

After two years, the Ochoas returned to Madrid so that Severo could take a teaching position at the University of Madrid, where he had studied. They moved into a house near the university, and Ochoa started to divide his time between teaching and doing research. Ochoa was now mainly interested in studying enzymes, and concentrated his work on them.

War in Spain

While the Ochoas were happy to return to Spain, the political situation continued to get worse. Finally, in 1936, civil war broke out between the Nationalists and the Republicans, the two sides fighting for control of the country. This was a terrible time to be in Spain. There was fighting in Madrid, and Ochoa sometimes saw dead people in the streets as he went to his laboratory. He asked Carmen if she thought they should leave the country. She said yes.

Escape from Spain

Luckily, Ochoa's former teacher, Dr. Negrín, who was then in the Republican government, helped the Ochoas get permission to leave Spain. But it would still be very difficult to get out of the country. They packed their bags and prepared to leave. Ochoa took all of his notes and some of his laboratory equipment. Carmen took apart a leather belt and sewed it together with seven thousand dollars inside—the money she had from her family. They were lucky to have enough money to get them to a safer country.

The Spanish Civil War 1936–1939

A civil war is a war between two groups in the same country, like the American Civil War, which was fought between the North and the South from 1861 to 1865.

In Spain, the instability of the early 1930s led to the Spanish Civil War. This war was fought from 1936 to 1939 by the Republicans, who wanted to maintain a liberal democracy, and the Nationalists, who wanted to form a conservative dictatorship. The war was very violent, resulting in the death of up to one million people.

The war ended in 1939, when the Nationalists took control of the country. Their leader, General Francisco Franco, started a dictatorship. A **dictator** is a ruler who does not give any power to the people of the country. A dictatorship is the opposite of a democracy, in which all people participate in the government of the country. The dictatorship of Franco lasted for almost 40 years. During this time, Spain was isolated from the other countries in Europe, which were against the dictatorship.

Severo and Carmen had to take a train to Valencia, and then another train to Barcelona. They had papers saying that they were allowed to leave the country for France, but they did not know how they would get there. In Barcelona, they met many people who were also trying to leave the country but had no way out.

Carmen was the one who got them out of the country. When they got to the offices where they needed to have their passports stamped, they found a long line of people waiting. Carmen did not get in line—she went right to the front and talked to the officials. She was very confident, and told them about the important people they knew, like Dr. Negrín. The officials stamped their passports and told them about a ship leaving for France the next day. Maybe they could get on it.

Severo and Carmen went to get on the ship, but first they had to go through customs. Customs is a point where people entering or leaving a country are checked, to make sure they are not taking anything with them that is not allowed. Severo and Carmen were nervous. Would the officials find the money Carmen had hidden in the belt? They didn't, which was a relief. But they looked at Ochoa's notes, full of scientific writing. The officials suspected that these were government secrets that Ochoa was stealing. But just then, Ochoa saw a person working there who he knew from Luarca. His friend explained who they were and let them through.

When Severo and Carmen got to the ship, they found that there were a couple of spaces left. They were finally going to get away! Ochoa had never felt such relief as he did at that moment. He later wrote, "Never in my life had I felt, and never again did I feel, the sense of freedom that I had when I stepped onto the deck of that boat. At that point, I realized what freedom really is, and what it really means."

The Ochoas arrived in France and took a train to Paris, where they met other Spanish **intellectuals** who had escaped from Spain. Intellectuals are people who are important because they have ideas that lead the thinking of a country. They spent a short time in Paris, while Ochoa tried to contact Dr. Meyerhof to ask whether he could go back to Germany and work with him again. Once he contacted him, Dr. Meyerhof agreed. Their friends warned them not to go, but Carmen thought it was very important that Ochoa continue his work, so they left for Germany in 1936.

The Ochoas' friends had warned them against going to Germany because they feared for Severo and Carmen's safety. A new government, led by Adolf Hitler, had taken control of the country. Hitler and his Nazi Party were against foreigners and Jews. A Jew is a person who practices the religion Judaism. The Nazis were forming a violent dictatorship. Many people in Europe were afraid that a big war was about to begin.

This picture is of Paris at around the time when Severo and Carmen lived there.

This is a photograph of Adolf Hitler in Nuremberg, Germany in 1938.

When they arrived in Heidelberg, Severo and Carmen found that many people had left Meyerhof's lab and fled the country. Dr. Meyerhof himself was worried because he was a Jew, and the Nazis wanted to kill all of the Jews or chase them out of Germany.

The German government was very suspicious of Severo and Carmen because they wanted to work and live with Jewish people. Their passports were taken away. However, Ochoa started his research in the laboratory, and Carmen spent her time learning German so she could talk to the family they were living with. But they were always worried about what was happening back home in Spain, where the civil war continued. And they worried about the situation in Germany, which was getting worse.

Leaving Germany

Dr. Meyerhof was worried about himself, but he was also worried about Severo and Carmen, and what would happen to them in Germany. He wrote to some scientists he knew in England and asked if they could arrange for Ochoa to go there and work. He got the answer he was hoping for. And so, at the beginning of the summer, Meyerhof left Germany for France, and the Ochoas left for England.

Oxford University is one of the most esteemed universities in the world. This photograph shows one of the university's many buildings.

Chapter 5:
Studies in England and the United States

Severo and Carmen went to Plymouth, England, where Severo continued his research at the Plymouth Marine Biological Laboratory. Ochoa was afraid that Carmen would be very lonely while he was working, so he convinced her to come to the laboratory and work as his assistant. She was hesitant at first, but she finally agreed. Carmen learned the laboratory work so quickly that Ochoa was amazed. After working together for a few months, they even published an article under the names of both of them! Despite the clouds of war hanging over Spain and the rest of Europe, it was a happy time for Severo and Carmen.

On to Oxford

After a year in Plymouth, Ochoa needed to find another job. He wanted to stay in England, so he was thrilled when he saw an advertisement for a position at Oxford University, working with a scientist named Rudolph Peters. Ochoa took the train to Oxford and interviewed with Peters, who said that unfortunately he was looking for someone with a different specialty than Ochoa. But they talked for a while, and Ochoa told him about all of the studies he had done with Dr. Meyerhof. Peters was so impressed that he offered to create another position especially for Ochoa! This was a wonderful opportunity.

Severo and Carmen moved to Oxford, and he started work. Dr. Peters was studying vitamin B1 and the functions it serves in the body, which Ochoa found very interesting. They worked very hard together and published many articles.

The Ochoas made many friends among the scientists at Oxford. They also met many other Spanish people who had come to England because of the war in their own country. They stayed in Oxford for two years, and were very happy.

World War II

However, once again came the darkness of war. World War II began, England and other countries went to war against Germany, and the Germans began to drop bombs on England. Almost all of the English scientists were asked to start helping with the war, but Ochoa, being a foreigner, was left out. He knew that they were in danger in England, and he asked Carmen what she thought about

World War II
1939–1945

World War II began in 1939 when the German army attacked Poland. By the time it was over in 1945, the war had involved nearly every part of the world. It was called the "second world war" because there had been a first world war fought between 1914 and 1918.

In the 1930s, the leaders of Germany, Italy, and Japan were military dictators. They wanted to increase the size and power of their own nations at the expense of other countries. Many countries opposed them, however, like Great Britain, France, the Soviet Union, and the United States.

The United States entered the war in 1941 after a Japanese attack on Pearl Harbor in Hawaii. The war ended shortly after the United States dropped two atomic bombs on Japan in 1945. These bombs caused the worst destruction anyone had ever seen.

Between 35 and 60 million people died in the war. Some six million of those people were Jews. The German dictator, Adolf Hitler, and his Nazi Party tried to destroy the Jewish people.

leaving for America. She thought it would be the best decision for Ochoa's career, and so they made plans to leave Europe.

The Ochoas left England in a convoy of ships that crossed the Atlantic Ocean. A convoy is a group of vehicles that travel together for safety. The crossing was dangerous, because they could have been attacked by German planes or ships, and there were **mines** in the water.

But they made it safely to Boston, and then New York. From there, they sailed to Mexico, where Ochoa's brother Luis had gone to escape the war in Spain. Before leaving England, Ochoa had contacted Carl and Gerty Cori, two scientists who worked at Washington University in Saint Louis, Missouri. The Coris invited the Ochoas to come to their lab, but Severo and Carmen had to wait until they got papers that allowed them to stay for a long period of time in the United States.

So they went to Mexico and waited for several weeks. Finally, the papers came, and they left for Saint Louis. When they arrived there, the Coris greeted them warmly, and took them in like son and daughter. They too had left Europe, twenty years earlier, and they could understand how Severo and Carmen felt. They understood that it is difficult to leave the country where you were born and move to a strange new place, especially when you are forced to do it by terrible circumstances like war.

Carl and Gerty Cori

Carl Cori and Gerty Radnitz were both born in Prague, in what is now the Czech Republic, in 1896. They went to medical school in Prague, where they met. In 1920, they both became doctors and got married. In 1922, they left for the United States, where they lived for the rest of their lives.

The Coris worked together as a team, researching sugars and starches in the body. Sugars and starches together are known as **carbohydrates**. They are the substances in the body that store energy. In 1936, the Coris made a very important discovery about how the body creates carbohydrates. For this discovery, they won the Nobel Prize in 1947.

Sadly, Gerty Cori died in 1957. From then on, Carl had to work alone. But he continued the studies that he had started with his wife until his death in 1984.

The Ochoas rented a small furnished apartment near the university. A furnished apartment has furniture already in it. This is what Carmen and Severo needed, since they had to leave almost all of their things in England. They liked Saint Louis, and thought was a very interesting and modern city with many cultural attractions and parks. Like most Europeans, Severo and Carmen liked to walk places, which Americans thought was strange. Even back then, people went everywhere in cars!

Ochoa enjoyed working with the Coris. He joined their team at Washington University, and helped with their research on enzymes and their effects on carbohydrates. The work was interesting, and the Coris were very kind. However, one day a letter arrived from a scientist in New York named Robert Goodhart. Ochoa had become friends with Goodhart back in Oxford. When Goodhart learned that the Ochoas were now in the United States, he wrote and asked Ochoa to come to New York University and open a laboratory of his own.

Ochoa did not know what to do. The Coris were treating him well, but he was working on their research, not his own. This would be an opportunity to study exactly what he wanted. He asked Carmen what he should do. She said it was time for Ochoa to become independent. For many years, he had worked with great scientists from whom he could learn. Now it was time for him to go out on his own and make his own discoveries.

After two years with the Coris, Severo and Carmen said goodbye and moved east to New York City. At the Medical School of New York University, Ochoa was given a small laboratory, where he began his own work on enzymes. He was very productive, and published many articles in the *Journal of Biological Chemistry*.

However, one day the directors of the medical school had decided that they needed the space for a new professor they had hired, leaving Ochoa with nowhere to go. Luckily, one of his friends, Dr. Isidor Greenwald, suggested that Ochoa join his laboratory in the Department of Biochemistry, also part of New York University. This suited Ochoa very well, and he was given a job as a professor of biochemistry.

Ochoa was put in charge of a small lab. For the first time, he had assistants to help him. These were young students who wanted to learn about biochemistry from him, the way he had learned from Dr. Juan Negrín twenty years before. One of these students was a young man named Arthur Kornberg, who was very bright. Within fifteen years, he would make a very important discovery himself.

Ochoa enjoyed working with these students, and they had a lot of respect for him. He taught them the most important qualities of a scientist—being careful, patient, thorough, and persistent. The students were very impressed with Ochoa's excitement about science. This excitement spread to them.

This is a photograph of Ochoa in his New York University lab in 1955.

Chapter 6:
The Nobel Prize

Severo and Carmen were enjoying the happiest period of their lives. In 1946, Ochoa was made a full professor at the university, which meant that he had a very high position. This made life easier for them.

Ochoa spent hours and hours in the laboratory, and his experiments produced many interesting results. He would come home in the evening and tell Carmen all about his work that day. She, in return, would tell him about her day, and they would talk about all sorts of things, from chemistry to literature. Carmen was his best friend. They also enjoyed doing things with their friends—mostly other scientists—and went to the theater or to concerts. Their life was simple but very satisfying.

This life continued for many years, with Ochoa making more and more discoveries in his lab about chemical processes in the body. In 1954, Ochoa became the head of the Department of Biochemistry at the university. He was now in charge of the whole department. He worked hard to make it the best department he could. Ochoa was very successful at this; the students learned a tremendous amount, and the professors continued to perform very successful experiments. Soon it was known as one of the best biochemistry departments in the country.

Becoming American Citizens

In 1956, two important things happened. First, Severo and Carmen became American citizens. That means that they officially became Americans, with the same rights as everybody else in the country. For example, they could now vote in elections and travel with an American passport. Severo and Carmen felt a great sense of gratitude toward the United States, which had taken them in when they were in need. Ochoa believed that it was their duty to recognize everything the country had done for them by becoming citizens.

A Discovery in Genetics

Another thing that happened that year was more important than it seemed at first. One of Ochoa's experiments on enzymes had an unexpected result. This discovery turned out to be very important in a type of science called **genetics**. Genetics is the study of the properties of different animals and plants, and how those properties are passed from one generation to the next. For example, if your parents both have blond hair, you are likely to have blond hair, but if neither of your parents has blond hair, you are unlikely to have blond hair. This is what the study of genetics involves.

Before the 1950s, scientists had discovered that substances called **DNA and RNA**, which are found in cells, held the secret for the design of living things. These "nucleic acids" tell the body how to create **proteins**, which are the main materials of all living things. Human DNA contains instructions for building humans, while monkey DNA contains instructions for building monkeys, daisy DNA contains information for building daisies, and so on. But nobody understood how DNA and RNA worked.

Ochoa discovered an enzyme, found in bacteria, to which he gave the long name "polynucleotide phosphorylase" (sounds like a tongue-twister, doesn't it?). While trying to figure out what the enzyme did, he learned that its purpose was to destroy RNA. But he also discovered that it was possible to reverse this process and use the enzyme to create RNA. This meant that people could experiment with creating proteins, and figure out how DNA and RNA work.

Ochoa realized this could be an important discovery, and he told other scientists about it right away. The news spread that someone had learned how to create proteins. This meant that scientists would be able to better understand how our bodies work, and might someday be able to use that knowledge to treat diseases. Soon Ochoa was well known for this discovery.

The Greatest Honor

Ochoa was very modest about his discovery, and told people that it was not certain that this discovery would have an important impact. He did not let his new fame go to his head or change his work. He simply continued working in his laboratory, although he did take time to go to some of the many conferences he was invited to.

And then one day in 1959, three years later, Ochoa arrived at his office and found that it was full of newspaper and television reporters. There was a rumor that he was going to win the Nobel Prize for Medicine—the biggest award in the world for a biologist! Ochoa couldn't believe it. Then, a message arrived—a telegram from Sweden. It was the Nobel committee, informing him that he had indeed won the Nobel Prize for his discovery about RNA! This is one of the greatest honors a scientist can receive.

Ochoa and his assistants cheered and drank champagne, while the reporters took their pictures. But the person Ochoa most wanted to share this news with, of course, was Carmen. He ran to his car and drove very fast toward his home. But he was going a little too fast, and he was stopped by a policeman! The policeman asked why he was speeding. Ochoa apologized, and said that he was speeding because he had just won the Nobel Prize. The policeman, astonished, let him go.

Ochoa and his students celebrate after learning that Ochoa had been awarded the Nobel Prize for Medicine.

For many weeks after that, Severo and Carmen received a flood of letters, phone calls, and visits from friends all over the world. They all wanted to congratulate Ochoa on his success, and tell him how proud they were. In Luarca, when the news was announced, they declared a holiday and let all the children go home from school.

The "Nobel Prize for Physiology or Medicine," as it is called, was given to both Ochoa and Arthur Kornberg, Ochoa's former student, who had made a discovery about DNA after leaving Ochoa's lab. Together, the two men's discoveries were a major step forward in understanding genetics.

A Trip to Stockholm

And so, a few weeks later, Severo and Carmen found themselves on a plane to Stockholm, the capital of Sweden. The Nobel Prizes are awarded in Stockholm by the King of Sweden himself. When the Ochoas arrived, they found the city to be very beautiful, covered in snow and full of lights and Christmas decorations. The city was filled with reporters from all over the world, who were there to write about the Nobel ceremony. And there were the winners of the other Nobel prizes for physics, chemistry, and literature. But most surprising to Ochoa was the large group of people who had traveled from Spain to watch him receive the award. Even the mayor of Luarca was there!

The awards ceremony took place in the Concert Hall of Stockholm. Hundreds of people gathered there, dressed in tuxedos and beautiful gowns. There were many intellectuals who had won the Nobel Prize in previous years. Just before the ceremony, a hush filled the room, and then in walked the King and Queen of Sweden. One by one, the award winners were called. Ochoa heard a speech being read about his achievements, and then the king handed him a gold medal and his award.

After the ceremony, there was a huge dinner in the City Hall for the prize winners and their friends and families. Ochoa sat between the queen and her daughter, the princess. Everyone made a speech. When his turn came, Ochoa thanked them for the award, and said, "This is indeed a great challenge which I will endeavor to meet with increased effort and dedication since the Nobel Prize is not the end of a path but the beginning of a new, and perhaps more arduous one."

Ochoa had spent the first half of his career learning from great scientists. Many of them had won the Nobel Prize: Santiago Ramón y Cajal, Otto Meyerhof, Rudolph Peters, Carl and Gerty Cori. Ochoa could hardly believe that he had now arrived at the same level of achievement as these people. He had become a great scientist!

The Happiest Moment

Back in their hotel room, after the Nobel Award ceremony, Severo and Carmen talked about the award. Carmen saw it as a reward for all the hard work that Ochoa had done in the laboratory. Ochoa said it was also a reward for Carmen, for all the sacrifices she had made. She had left Spain to follow Ochoa, and had dedicated her life to helping him succeed. Now, there could be no doubt that it was worth it. They agreed that this was the happiest moment of their lives.

This photograph of Severo and Carmen was taken at a reception before the Nobel Prize Awards Ceremony in 1959.

Chapter 7:
Celebration and Loss

The Ochoas went back to New York, and Severo continued with his work. He was now a famous scientist, and more dedicated to his work than ever.

As the years went by, Ochoa published more and more articles on his discoveries, and he received more awards and honors. The greatest one came almost twenty years after he won the Nobel Prize. The government of Madrid announced plans to create a brand-new center for the study of biology: The Severo Ochoa Center for Molecular Biology. They asked him whether he would consider coming back to Spain to work there.

Returning to Spain

Ochoa considered this for a few years, while the institute was being built. He made many trips to Spain, and started working with medical researchers there. Finally, in 1985, when Ochoa was 80 years old, he and Carmen decided to move back to Spain. Carmen had always missed Spain, which she loved. They had left the country 50 years earlier, thinking they would never again live there. Now, they decided it was time to go home.

Ochoa returned to Spain a hero. He was awarded the Ramón y Cajal Prize, Spain's highest award for medicine. He and Carmen moved to Madrid, where they had lived 50 years earlier. They had been happy in the United States, a country they loved, but they were excited to be back in Spain after so long.

Tragedy

But suddenly, tragedy struck. One day, a few months after their return, Carmen said she did not feel well. They went to a doctor, who said she had some heart problems, but they were not too serious. A few days later, Ochoa was in the kitchen when he heard Carmen call his name in the bedroom. He ran to the room, and found her lying on the bed. She had died.

Ochoa lived for seven more years, but he was lost without Carmen. She had been an essential part of his life and his work. He was overcome with grief. He decided to give up his work completely. As he said, "My life without Carmen is no life at all." She meant more to him than all of his achievements as a scientist.

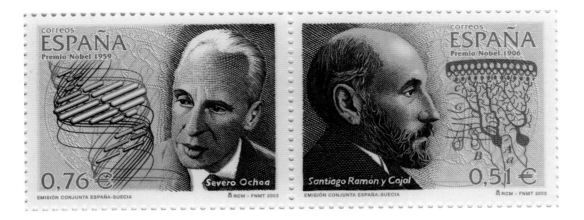

These are special edition stamps that were released in 2003 to honor past Nobel Prize winners such as Severo Ochoa and Santiago Ramón y Cajal.

Ochoa's Legacy

Severo Ochoa is remembered today as one of the great scientists of the twentieth century. He was a founding father of biochemistry, and a leader in genetic research. He showed the world what someone can achieve with a love of science and the dedication to work hard.

In His Own Words

Severo Ochoa's advice to young students:

"If you have a passion for science, become scientists. Don't worry about what will become of you. If you work hard and with enthusiasm, science will fill your lives."

Glossary

biochemistry study of the chemistry of living things, in particular the tiny structures in the body called cells

biologist person who studies biology

biology study of living things, such as humans, animals, and plants

carbohydrates sugars and starches–the substances in the body that store energy

chemistry study of chemical substances and the changes that take place when they combine with one another

conference large meeting of people who study the same thing, so that they can make presentations to each other and exchange information about their discoveries

degree title that a college or university gives to a student when his or her studies are completed

determination having an objective and following it through

dictator ruler who does not give any power to the people of the country; his or her government is called a dictatorship

DNA and RNA substances found in the body that carry instructions for the design of different plants and animals; DNA and RNA are studied in genetics

enzyme substance in the body that speeds up chemical reactions, such as the digestion of food

experimental biology study of how the body works, done by performing experiments in laboratories

genetics study of similarities and differences in how living creatures and plants reproduce their own kind; this science studies how tiny units called genes carry information from generation to generation

intellectual person who is important because he or she has ideas that lead the thinking of a country

medical researcher type of doctor who does experiments in laboratories

mines explosive devices

physics study of physical objects and the way they are moved by energy

physician type of doctor who treats patients

proteins building blocks and main materials of all living things

Timeline

1905   Severo Ochoa is born in Luarca, Spain on September 24.

1912   Father dies, and family moves to Málaga, in the south of Spain.

1921   Finishes high school and decides to study medicine and become a medical researcher; moves to Madrid to study at the university.

1927   Works in Scotland with Dr. Noel Paton; writes his first article for publication in a scientific journal.

1929   Goes to Germany to work with Dr. Otto Meyerhof; takes his first trip to the U.S.; graduates and becomes a doctor.

1930   Returns to Spain and meets Carmen Cobián; they marry in 1931.

1932   Begins two-year stay in England to work with the scientists Harold Dudley and Sir Henry Dale.

1934   Returns to Madrid to work at the University of Madrid.

1936   The Spanish Civil War begins. The Ochoas escape from Spain to France, then to Germany; they return to Dr. Meyerhof's lab.

1937   The Ochoas leave Germany for England to escape from the Nazis.

1940   The Ochoas leave England to escape World War II and arrive in the U.S.; Ochoa begins work with Carl and Gerty Cori in St. Louis.

1942   The Ochoas move to New York; Severo works at NY University.

1956   The Ochoas become American citizens.

1959   Ochoa is awarded the Nobel Prize for Medicine.

1985   The Ochoas return to Spain.

1986   Carmen Ochoa dies.

1993   Severo Ochoa dies.

Further Information

Further Reading

Allan, Tony. *Understanding DNA: A Breakthrough in Medicine*. Chicago: Heinemann Library, 2002.

Baldwin, Joyce. *DNA Pioneer: James Watson and the Double Helix*. New York: Walker & Company, 1994.

Hunter, Shaun. *Leaders in Medicine*. New York: Crabtree Publishing Company, 1999.

St. John, Jetty. *Hispanic Scientists*. Bloomington, MN: Capstone Press, 1996.

Addresses

UCSC Center for the Molecular Biology of RNA
420 Sinsheimer Labs, UCSC
Santa Cruz, CA 95064

Society of Mexican American Engineers and Scientists
MAES, Inc.
711 W. Bay Area Blvd., Suite #206
Webster, TX 77598-4051

Index